How to Finance a Marijuana Business

Cannabis Meets Crowdfunding

Author: Douglas Slain, J.D., M.A.

Preface

"The illegality of cannabis is outrageous, an impediment to full utilization of a drug which helps produce the serenity and insight, sensitivity and fellowship so desperately needed in this increasingly mad and dangerous world."

— Carl Sagan

Table of Contents

Lecture One: The End of Prohibition

Today medical marijuana is legal in twenty-one states and Washington D.C.

As of now, four states, Colorado, Washington, Alaska, Oregon and Washington D. C., legalized marijuana for recreational purposes.

Two states, Colorado and Washington, legalized marijuana for recreational purposes in late 2013. Oregon did the same in 2014.

Other states, including New York, New Jersey, and Arizona, are considering plans to legalize medical marijuana and, eventually, recreational marijuana.

The marijuana industry is not just a matter of direct product sales, already estimated to be in the billions of dollars. The market also incorporates any number of ancillary businesses ranging from consulting to marketing to the manufacturing of vaporizers and security systems to seed-to-sale software systems that track inventory.

Many still argue that the industry is not ready for prime time insofar as Federally-chartered institutions continue to be understandably reluctant to accept deposits. Similarly, institutional investors are still mostly sitting it out, waiting for some resolution on the Federal level.

There are remaining vocal opponents to the whole industry and some feel legalization is bad public policy. "This is big tobacco-redux," says Kevin Sabet, director of Drug Policy Institute at the University of Florida and a former official with the Office of National Drug Control Policy. "They know the only way to make money is to create addiction."

Jeffrey Miron, a senior fellow at the Cato Institute, favors decriminalization but warns, "The door is slightly ajar but not enough to let the horses gallop out." Miron believes that the marijuana industry should be treated as the tobacco and liquor industries but feels the classification of cannabis as a felony-level drug cannot be ignored and he suggests deep caution at this time.

However, Sabet's and Miron's views are becoming increasingly in the minority. A recent Gallop poll showed that 58 percent of Americans are in favor of recreational marijuana becoming legal, while an even larger percentage are in favor of legalizing medical marijuana.

Three 2014 developments signal a new regulatory regime is on the way.

1) The U.S. Department of Justice announced it will not interfere with marijuana retail sales as long as all state and Federal rules are followed and all taxes are paid.

2) The U.S. Treasury Department's Financial Crimes Enforcement Network issued formal guidance to U.S. banks on how to do business with marijuana firms.

3) The President of the United States mentioned marijuana and alcohol in the same sentence.

An enormous, quasi-dormant underground economy is awakening and large components are coming to the surface. Taylor West, deputy director of the 440-member National Cannabis Industry Association, said, "There is a whole canopy of products that goes beyond plants." He cites cannabis-infused foods and drinks, cannabis oils, butters, tinctures, and salves.

New regulatory demands will spark other opportunities such as laboratories to test for impurities and software systems to track product from seed-to-sale. But make no mistake about it: Some investors in some of the publicly-held cannabis-connected companies detailed at hempinsiders.com will lose money.

In early 2014 several marijuana companies quadrupled in value on the OTC Board in a matter of weeks; some of them were accused of pump and dump schemes. FINRA has announced that it has seen a number of red flags among public cannabis companies. It also pointed to the fact that a CEO of one firm was once indicted for a Ponzi scheme.

Lecture Two: Reasons to Invest

IJK

The most obvious signal that a new, legal multi-billion dollar industry was becoming a reality was the passage of marijuana recreational laws in Colorado and Washington in late 2013. For the first time, marijuana prohibition finally ended in two states, creating badly-needed sources of state and local tax revenue. Tax revenues from sales of medical marijuana had already found a welcome and eager reception from other state and local municipalities; now in Washington, Colorado, Oregon, Alaska and Washington DC there will be even more tax revenue.

A less obvious but possibly more important development was a comment by President Obama where he compared marijuana to alcohol, or at least he mentioned them in the same context. Although Obama was alluding to our nation's social ills, many observers came away with the impression that, finally, some form of Federal prohibition of marijuana is on its way, with state regulation and state and local taxation to follow.

Another sign of a maturing industry is that there are now funding portals, permitted under new SEC rules (following the JOBS Act), that facilitate private placement investments in cannabis start-ups and expansions.

Cannabis investors and entrepreneurs now meet online with little or no cost of intermediation. There is no longer any need to pay membership fees to join an investor-entrepreneur group.

Capital wants to flow in and new companies want to start or expand and, while nothing has changed in the eyes of Federal law, "prohibition premium" opportunities still exist because *everything has changed in eyes of Federal law enforcement.*

Since promulgation of the Cole Memo (discussed in detail in Lecture Four and appearing as an appendix to this handbook) marijuana businesses finally have easy-to-follow Federal rules and regulations. Follow all the rules and pay your taxes and you are OK with the Federal government: that is the message.

Lecture Three: Market Opportunities

Many believe that when marijuana finally becomes truly legal, when cannabis and hemp prohibition finally end, together they will generate close to $50 billion in annual sales. To put this into perspective, the U.S. beer market is $100 billion annually; the wine market is $32 billion.

This $50 billion number incorporates approximately $15 billion that will remain grey market and therefore untaxable. But the remaining $35 billion of taxable revenue does not even include the billions more in taxable revenue that will be generated by ancillary businesses discussed in this book.

On top of this, there is the burgeoning industrial hemp industry as well as new markets for edibles, tinctures, oils and salves. The consumer packaged goods business is an industry where the business itself increases as new products are introduced, and the marijuana industry is exploding with a range of new product lines.

Although taxes are higher with recreational marijuana than with medical marijuana and although the medical marijuana market is being cannibalized in part by the recreational market, the aggregate marijuana market will be significantly larger than the former medical marijuana market alone.

Also, the general legal market continues to expand in a number of ways outside its former medical marijuana limitations.

In Colorado, new customers include tourists and non-medical marijuana residents who no longer have to buy from "friends who have friends" who may have enjoyed medical marijuana status.

The prediction in a fully functional Washington state marketplace is for $1 billion in annual taxable revenue; some claim that number will represent less than half the total revenue, however, as many residents will continue to make use of the black market in part just to avoid the added costs resulting from multiple layers of taxation and by state and local municipalities. There is also concern that Washington regulations impose an unrealistically small amount of space for indoor cultivation—creating supply side limitations. In addition, Washington, for now, is permitting only 334 licensed retail facilities—woefully inadequate in the view of many.

California initiated the legalization of marijuana in 1996 when it began offering medical marijuana cards and allowing dispensaries and delivery services. Twenty-three more states and the District of Columbia followed. Treatable conditions include chronic pain, stress disorders, glaucoma, and chemotherapy-related illnesses.

However, as everyone knows, the vast majority of cannabis consumers have used it, not for any medicinal reason in particular, but for the same reason they drink wine or beer, to achieve a "buzz"—that is to say to alter their consciousness mildly. One advantage of recreational marijuana is that users do not need expensive annually-renewable medical marijuana licenses often based on spurious medical conditions.

State laws differ widely. In general, states with the most stable market places also have the most regulation.

Lecture Four: The Cole Memorandum

Marijuana may be illegal in the eyes of the Federal government but it has become less illegal.

In August 2013 the U.S. Justice Department released a memorandum written by Deputy Attorney General James M. Cole, clarifying the Federal government's approach to marijuana cultivation, distribution, and sales. Known as the "Cole Memo," the document offers formal guidance to the states that have legalized medical marijuana and recreational marijuana.

The Justice Department will not pursue criminal charges against marijuana-related businesses that follow Federal, state, and local rules and regulations. The Cole Memo instructs prosecutors to bring marijuana-related prosecutions in only eight instances:

1) Sales to minors
2) Revenue going to criminal enterprises
3) Sales across state lines
4) Sales in connection with other drugs
5) Violence
6) Use of Federal land
7) DUIs

The Cole Memo, for the first time, gives marijuana businesses a clear cut frame-work of rules and regulations to follow regarding exposure to Federal prosecutors. As said above, doing business in the marijuana industry may still be illegal, but it is a lot less illegal than it used to be.

Previously, the Ogden Memo of 2009 was never intended to shield cannabis from federal enforcement action and prosecution, even where those activities that purport to comply with state law. Persons who are in the business of cultivating, selling or distributing marijuana, and those who knowingly facilitate such activities, are in violation of the Controlled Substances Act, regardless of state law, under the Ogden Memo.

With that understanding, the Cole Memo provides an illuminating laundry list of federal enforcement priorities, to better focus its limited resources:

1) Preventing the distribution of marijuana to minors;

2) Preventing revenue from the sale of marijuana from going to criminal enterprises, gangs, and cartels;

3) Preventing the diversion of marijuana from states where it is legal under state law in some form to other states;

4) Preventing state-authorized marijuana activity from being used as a cover or pretext for the trafficking of other illegal drugs or other illegal activity;

5) Preventing violence and the use of firearms in the cultivation and distribution of marijuana;

6) Preventing drugged driving and the exacerbation of other adverse public health consequences associated with marijuana use;

7) Preventing the growing of marijuana on public lands and the attendant public safety and environmental dangers posed by marijuana production on public lands; and

8) Preventing marijuana possession or use on federal property.

As long as states do nothing to impair these federal priorities, such as preventing drugged driving, by "implementing strong and effective regulatory and enforcement systems," the feds are good with whatever states decide to do.

If state enforcement efforts are not sufficiently robust to protect against these harms, the federal government may seek to challenge the regulatory structure itself in addition to continuing to bring individual enforcement actions, including criminal prosecutions, focused on those harms.

As with the Department's previous statements on this subject, the Cole memorandum is intended solely as a guide to the exercise of investigative and prosecutorial discretion. The memorandum does not alter in any way the

Department's authority to enforce federal law, including federal laws relating to marijuana, regardless of state law.

Neither the guidance herein nor any state or local law provides a legal defense to a violation of federal law, including any civil or criminal violation of the CSA.

Even in jurisdictions with strong and effective regulatory systems, evidence that particular conduct threatens federal priorities will subject that person or entity to federal enforcement action, based on the circumstances. The memorandum may not be relied upon to create any rights, substantive or procedural, enforceable at law by any party in any matter civil or criminal. It applies prospectively to the exercise of prosecutorial discretion in future cases and does not provide defendants or subjects of enforcement action with a basis for reconsideration of any pending civil action or criminal prosecution.

Lecture Five: Colorado versus Washington

Which state is going to serve as a model for other markets when the time comes to craft each state's recreational cannabis regime, Colorado or Washington? Although Washington and Colorado both legalized recreational marijuana in November 2013, they have taken different paths.

From a business perspective, Colorado's recreational market has become a national sensation, generating millions in sales and millions in taxable revenue.

Washington state, on the other hand, has yet to even open for business. Further, state regulators appeared to be their own worst enemies when they recently reduced the number of licenses for which any single business can apply. They also recently reduced the square footage permitted each grower. These changes have created serious problems for businesses that had already invested time and money on earlier assumptions.

"People are apoplectic," Washington state attorney Ryan Agnew said. "Many people had already formed partnerships and made the capital outlays necessary to grow at the higher production cap."

As if the above were not bad enough, some Washington state regulators apparently are not planning on sizeable amounts of taxable revenue until Mid-2015, according to several insider reports. This would be a full year later than originally announced, although some sources stress that this reflects a worst case scenario.

"The MMJ community was cut out of the drafting of the law and thus missed an opportunity to share their knowledge of the market and work in rules that might benefit existing MMJ businesses," Agnew said, mentioning location restrictions and tax levels in particular.

Significantly, Colorado had been careful to create a clear and strong regulatory framework that already covered medical marijuana, and that regulatory framework was in place when the legislators turned their attention to recreational cannabis. Many observers attribute the success of the Colorado "experiment" to this fact, for starters. Washington, by comparison, still is in a muddle with medical marijuana; while the legislators argue about rules governing dispensaries, the medical marijuana industry in the state is generally illegal (and is tolerated as such).

Who knows? Problems could eventually develop in Colorado if unrestrained growth and publicity invites scrutiny from Federal prosecutors. Maybe Washington's model, starting in 2015, may become the national model, after smoothing out its initial challenges.

Many believe that Washington's interest in eliminating, rather than restructuring, the medical marijuana industry will prove to be a crucial mistake, at least in the short and mid-term.

Colorado left the industry in the hands of the free market. There are an unlimited number of retail licenses (although the number is on hold for now until they get up to speed) and an unlimited number of grow sites. And residents can grow their own legally.

For now at least, other states considering recreational marijuana legalization will want to look at Colorado for a business model.

Lecture Six: The Future of Recreational Marijuana

What can you expect now? Following Washington and Colorado, what is next? What states are looking good?

Look for states that:

- Launch a medical marijuana initiative ballot drive or state-wide general election to implement a medical marijuana program that is fully regulated and taxed; then,
- Create awareness in the state's citizenry that the medical marijuana industry is viably regulated, taxed and provides a state and local tax base; then,
- Pass a recreational marijuana ballot or legislation, with regulations and a tax regime, and addressing packaging, seed-to-sales monitoring, and distance regulations.

Do not look for states likely to over-regulate in their zeal for the public weal.
Here are the key issues:

- Taxation

This is obviously a source of tension: Most taxes are passed on to users and too much taxation can lead to users returning to the black market, leading to fewer sales and less tax revenue. The same principal applies to regulation by states and local governments: an excess of rules to follow will impede sales and cut into tax revenue. Most observers believe that Washington's taxes are already too high; some complain about Colorado's taxes.

On the other hand, high taxes can help establish the industry's attractiveness and legitimacy as well as lead other states to enact recreational marijuana legislation. Again, though, this impact has to be balanced with the reality that there is a large black market already offering a known and valued product *sans* any price increases attributable to taxes and the cost of complying with regulations.

For local governments, tax revenues are a strong incentive to not implement moratoriums. Look for local governments that are receptive to new taxes in lieu of enacting moratoriums on the business.

- Limitations on outlets and licenses

Washington's regulatory scheme limits the number of retail outlets and grow operations. It also limits the number of licenses allocated to one person or firm. This has had a negative impact on production efficiencies and proposed chain operations are now considered unrealistic. All of these measures work in favor of an already strong black market.

- Limitations on infused edibles

Some states are considering laws that will prohibit infused products with more than a specified amount of THC per gram. Such legislation could dampen hash sales and also cut into the sales of oils and salves.

- Non-profits

Medical marijuana businesses are typically non-profits. If recreational marijuana regulatory schemes follow that model it will cut into available outside capital.

- Distances

State regulations specify how to incorporate rules governing the minimum distance between retail outlets and schools, public parks, and other places. These regulations will impact real estate decisions.

- Seed-to-sale tracking

Seed-to-sale software tracks plants from the moment of propagation to the moment of sale. This is a low-cost means of reassuring state regulators and Federal prosecutors that the product is not crossing over to the black market, for one instance.

Lecture Seven: Top 10 Problems

- BANKING

Banks, as Federally-chartered institutions in the U.S., have always been an Achilles heel for marijuana businesses. Banks do not allow debit or credit accounts and they do not accept checking or savings accounts.

That being said, this is another area where there is recent good news. In early 2014 U.S. Attorney General Eric Holder announced that the Justice Department and the Treasury Department were jointly working on ways for banks to work with the marijuana industry.

- TAXATION DEDUCTIONS

U.S. Code section 280E reads:

"No deduction or credit shall be allowed for any amount paid or incurred during the taxable year in carrying on any trade or business if such trade or business or the activities which comprise such trade or business consists of trafficking in controlled substances within the meaning of schedule I and II of the Controlled Substance Act which is prohibited by Federal law or the law of any State in which such trade or business is conducted."

Although marijuana is a schedule I controlled substance under Federal law, the above tax code section is a problem. However, the IRS v. CHAMP case, for one, offers some relief. This is definitely an area where you want to consult with a tax professional.

- CAPITAL FORMATION

It takes money to make money, generally speaking.

Access to capital is essential for any start-up and for many expansions of a business. Traditionally, small start-up marijuana businesses have relied on friends and family for funding until breakeven.

In late 2013, the SEC changed a law that has been in existence for over 80 years, allowing marijuana start-ups (among all other start-ups) the opportunity to raise money with equity crowd funding. The SEC's new rule 506(c has made it possible for marijuana investors and entrepreneurs to meet online at funding portals with minimal intermediation costs. Marijuana entrepreneurs can now find funding portals and other online resources that will both lend money and make equity investments.

Prior to the Cole Memo, most investments were privately placed with only ancillary businesses. Now, most investments remain privately placed but they can be made directly into the industry, where most of the money is being made.

- Regulations

Recreational marijuana is highly regulated with a consequent burden of paperwork and business organization. Software designed for these purposes is available and competing software is on its way.

- Local governance

Municipalities are typically given leeway under state Constitutions to do what they want. Any municipality can enact a moratorium on anything to do with marijuana any time it wishes.

States with a track record of successfully regulating medical marijuana (and recreational marijuana) offer better opportunities for avoiding moratoriums.

If you are considering a dispensary business, remember that, although 21 states have enacted medical marijuana regimes, only 12 of them allow dispensaries. The other 9 states allow caretaker and patient growing. Some states are in the early legislative stages of initiating a dispensary system. States with existing dispensary laws are the following: Arizona, California, Colorado, District of Columbia, Maine, New Jersey, New Mexico, Rhode Island, and Vermont.

States that have passed medical marijuana dispensary laws which are not yet operative are the following: Connecticut, Delaware, Illinois, Massachusetts, Nevada, and New Hampshire.

States that in fact "allow" dispensaries without legal recognition include the following: Michigan, Montana, Oregon and Washington.

- Human Resources

MARIIJUANA is still not a word most job applicants feature on their resume. While bud-tenders are not shy in using the word, many lawyers, CPAs, and marketing professionals are typically not eager for a professional "dope" connection.

The good news is that this general perception of cannabis and cannabis-related products and activities is changing rapidly and radically. Clinical trials pointing to the efficacy of cannabis in any number of ailments and illnesses are legend. Edibles, oils and salves are becoming more popular for a variety of reasons. With edibles there is no ignition and heat in the lungs.

- Prices

Prices will be driven by production and competition, and taxation, in that order. Profit margins to date are more than adequate.

- Late to the party?

In truth, the national industry is at the beginning of the end of prohibition of cannabis in almost all its forms and many, many opportunities will present themselves over the next few years.

- Black Market

The only real competition to licensed marijuana sales is the black market. In fact, one much criticized study concluded that the licensed sector of the industry in that state, following legalization of recreational marijuana, will only amount to 25% of the total market, due to taxes and the cost of complying with regulations.

Black market sources can offer the convenience of home delivery with hours tailored to the user. All the expenses of safety testing, seed-to-sale tracking, taxes, packaging costs, and administrative costs do not have to be included in the sales price.

Talking points for paying the extra fare include:

- Lab-tested quality
- Wider range of product
- Hard to find strain, edibles and CBD products
- Paraphernalia available for sale
- No laws being broken
- Security

Marijuana crimes continue to rise. Both cash and product are valuable. Install good security systems and do NOT have a fire arm on the premises.

Lecture Eight: State-by-State Status

Alaska

Approved a regulatory scheme similar to Colorado's business model. State taxes will be $50/oz.

Oregon

There are over 200 unregulated but tolerated medical dispensaries in Oregon. Changes are underway.

New Hampshire

The House approved medical marijuana in early 2014; stay tuned.

Rhode Island

Rhode Island has passed medical marijuana laws and decriminalized small amounts of marijuana.

California

The defeat of Proposition 9 in 2012 means many sponsors want to wait until 2016 when they can execute an aggressive media campaign. However, California could move forward sooner; it has 2 legislative initiatives underway.

Arizona

In December 2012 state-licensed dispensaries began to open. There is much municipal hostility in this conservative state, but the smart money is on increased legalization.

Maine

Maine residents have voted 60% to 40% in favor of legalization.

Massachusetts

Massachusetts passed a medical marijuana program in 2012 that they are still implementing.

Nevada

Nevada is on schedule to become the first state to recognize out-of-state cards at its licensed medical marijuana dispensaries.

Vermont

Vermont opened its first dispensaries in 2014 with strong market potential from tourists throughout New England.

New York

While there is wide-spread support for both medical and recreational marijuana, legalization is several years away.

Florida

While the aging population and tourism have led to a healthy recreational market, any bills to legalize marijuana died in early 2015.

Delaware

The first dispensary opened in late 2014.

Lecture Nine: Key Takeaways

When your state is in the process of deciding to legalize marijuana, it will be important to lobby for measures to permit growers, prosecutors, edible makers, and infused product bakers and other processors to prepare for retail openings; otherwise the public's first experience will be one of long lines, limited product, and perhaps accusations of "price gouging."

Assuming your state follows Colorado's business model, which was to give recreational licenses to existing medical marijuana dispensaries and then to restrict recreational inventory to what could be transferred from existing medical marijuana dispensaries, you will have to synchronize the growth cycle of the plants with the a store opening so you will have adequate numbers of plants ready to trim.

You will want to check with wholesalers or growers to see if they can handle additional supply demands, and which strains they can offer.

You definitely want to stock up on edibles and other specialty products. Dried marijuana flowers are easily found on the black market, but specialty products are not. New recreational marijuana users will be especially attracted to edibles and vaporizers. You want to create a one-stop opportunity for all things cannabis.

If you do run low on a particular popular product it is better to put a limit per customer before running out altogether.

You may want to develop a web site and/or a brochure that details what is behind your pricing policy. You can broadly or specifically discuss your cost of doing business, including multiple taxation, cost of seed-to-sale tracking, value of hard-to-find strains, and even employee benefits.

Cash-only signage should be at the front counter. Consider installing an ATM machine if practicable.

Have a Facebook page with a Twitter ID on your front door and business cards. Use customer lists to develop a social network to keep customers up-to-date on specials and other offerings.

Stay current with your store's listings and reviews on retail finder services such as Leafly and Weedmaps.

We strongly encourage association with homeopathic and palliative companies and products. Cannabis and wellness are increasingly becoming associated in the public's mind. You could chose something particularly appropriate for arthritis, for instance.

If you have the right email lists, emails and email alerts are the most powerful form of social networking. For instance, send routine Friday noon emails offering something special, especially a new edible.

Create a loyalty program that requires an email address. Have business cards and an online presence with name, logo, business hours, location(s), and contact information.

Invest in professional packaging or in a middleman for that purpose.

Regarding your store's physical footprint, depending on the available real estate stock for this purpose, recreational marijuana retailers will not want to follow the template of the medical marijuana stores, where there is usually a large waiting room. You do not want to have a waiting room! However, you will want a small counter to meet people inside the front door.

Script your store's recorded phone message, and have someone record it. Update frequently. (It just sounds good).

Invest in software. Ask seed-to-sale software vendors for contact information of current customers or at least contact information for at least one customer. Ask if you can give the software a trial run before signing a long-term contract. You need to be working with at least one software sale representative regarding your business. Your software vendor(s) can help you develop and improve your business and share what others are doing. Software vendors report that clients under-value their information.

Flexibility is the key. First, have a solid plan for pricing and products. Second, decide how to let people know about you. Third, stay in good standing with regulators of all stripes. Fourth and finally, plan for the future. Try to have an annual plan in place from day one, including promotions, staffing and training, inventory, and software.

Lecture Ten: Cannabis Niches

Commercial Cultivation

Some growers produce medium to large scale amounts of cannabis for sale to wholesalers, retailers, and edible manufacturers. A few grow outdoors but most grow indoors, to protect the females, control the environment, and grow multiple harvests.

After propagation, usually done with cloning, the plants are graduated to larger pots as they grow. In seed-to-sale states, each newly cloned plant is considered a seed. After harvesting, processing includes drying, trimming, and packaging. Other steps, taken less frequently, include lab testing and oil extraction. In states with vertical integration laws, retailers may be asked to grow some if not all of their inventory.

Cultivation is an attractive market segment because recreational marijuana requires a lot of inventory and growers can generate substantial incomes. Some growers use interstate commerce to maximize profits—and risks. An entire grey market has sprung up to create packaging for use with the postal service, Federal Express, and other carriers.

Recreational demand has opened up the industry like nothing before it, and the future is for more of the same. Also, there is greater demand for edibles, extract products, salves and oils.

Professional grade extraction equipment costs thousands of dollars and most of our clients have used private placements or PIPRs (Private Issuers Publicly Raising) forums for raising funds to purchase the equipment.

Are organics in the future?

The recreational marijuana markets in particular are ripe for organically grown products. The propagation of seedlings or clones under organic rules can be challenging at first so some growers may be tempted to offer "organic" product that did not begin organic.

Cultivators can focus on mass market strains (a "Miller High Life" strain) which appeals to the masses and has a fast gestation period, for lower prices. The connoisseur crowd may be interested in specialty strains and will pay more for them.

Some growers are already specializing in "clone factories," which facilitate growers who want to react to a particular market demand.

Cultivation costs include fees and licenses required by the state as well as the cost of the growing space, plus equipment. Permits and licenses can range into the thousands of dollars. Cost of electricity for large indoor grows can be very high, prompting use of generators in some remote locations.

Warehouse space needs to be procured for the growing area, and then thousands of dollars are required to build, insulate, ventilate and cool rooms within the larger space for vegetative and flowering stages. Light fixtures, bulbs, seed and plants and other equipment must be purchased. Tracking systems, processing equipment, and security systems are all a part of start-up costs.

For labor, you can expect to pay $45,000 for a head grower and up to $14/hour for other employees or trimming contractors, perhaps more.

Professional services include legal, insurance, and accounting.

The biggest risks are associated with breaking the law, such as selling to minors or selling across state lines. Regulators may want to inspect to see the grow area is what you say it is (and it may be tempting to not disclose everything).

Growers are generally able to raise money from private offerings to friend, family and small angel investors, or through online equity crowdfunding platforms. Generally debt investments are available at a steep 20% annual return. Equity investments are negotiable.

Advantages to cultivation include a low bar to entry. After procuring the necessary state licenses, a cultivation entrepreneur can easily bring an operation up to speed by hook or by crook. Commercial botany knowledge is very helpful.

As long as the Federal government does not roll over to the tobacco lobby, marijuana cultivation will remain a regional business.

Many if not most growers come from the black market, others come from commercial cultivation of other types of foods.

Retail

In the medical marijuana field, retail outlets are commonly called dispensaries. Just as with recreational marijuana, these outlets sell paraphernalia, such as pipes and bongs, as well as an array of other products such different vaporizers, edibles, infused chocolates, and other ancillary products.

The location of store or dispensaries is determined by local ordinances including those limitation distances to schools and parks. In some states, retailers will be required to grow some or all of the product sold.

Regulations of resale businesses will govern how they can advertise, manage inventory and hire employees or contractors.

There is strong demand for resale outlets, but unfortunately their number and size is limited by legal considerations rather than market realities.

Recreational outlets should do substantially more business than medical marijuana dispensaries.

The biggest risk a retailer takes is the risk of selling to minors or being involved in an interstate transaction. Other risks or downsides include local moratoriums or planning changes, limited real estate supply, zoning laws, high rent costs, employee theft, cash management and accounting, black market competition (what else is new?), tax audits, inventory management including picking the right strains and maintaining supply chain management, and staff training. It is a business, after all.

How about access to capital?

U.S. banks will not be lending to marijuana-associated businesses any time soon. The SBA is not going to step up to the plate, either. Retailers therefore have to be self-funded or funded with private placements or private offerings.

Interestingly, a whole new industry has recently arrived felicitously with the early stage of the end of marijuana prohibition: equity crowd funding, discussed in Lecture Twelve of this book.

Some private placements are limited to in-state residents. With loans, retailers are paying as much as 25%; with equity, retailers are negotiating the best terms they can get and afford.

Retailers can grow a customer base quickly in a recreational market and secure a market share before larger competition enters the field. If the Federal government ends prohibition of cannabis and hemp, retailers will have an opportunity to quickly spread into other states.

Edibles and Infused Products

This market segment consists of cannabis food, brownies and other deserts, oils, hashish, drinks, tinctures, waxes which are sometimes referred to as "tabs," salves, and other products. These are products that contain THC. Cannabinoids (CBDs) are other chemicals that have been extracted from cannabis plants by means a variety of methods.

THC-based products contain psychoactive components and are used for recreational purposes.

CBD-based products do not contain THC and are generally used for health-related purposes.

Large paraphernalia companies are located in Germany, the Netherlands, the U.K., and other European countries, competing with major brands in the U.S. Several vaporizer pen manufacturers are competing actively for market share.

Testing Laboratories

Testing laboratories put cannabis and cannabis-infused edibles and other products through a variety of tests to determine THC content and contamination from mold, fungus and pesticides. Many laboratories also offer research and development services such as measuring CBDs for growers looking to produce strains of greater interest to some of their client base.

Also in this market are testing technology companies which offer specialized equipment and supplies to retail testing laboratories.

Growth is guaranteed in an expanding recreational marijuana economy because regulations will require testing. Right now, there are only a few up and running laboratories in each area of the country. New players in this space may want to aim to dominate an under-served market before taking on a well-served geographical area.

Not including staff, start-up costs can exceed $100,000. Faint of heart or light of wallet need not apply. Just renting the equipment can cost between $50,000 and $250,000/annum. A young skilled scientist will cost at least $75,000. Then follows the costs of solvents and chemicals used for testing. Finally, there are the costs of state certification and licensing fees.

States that legalize recreational marijuana do not have to require testing, but everyone understandably assumes they will do so.

Other negatives are the possibility of fire, explosions, and harm to the environment caused by the solvents and chemicals being used.

Some good news is that conventional financing is available. As cannabis continues to lose its stigma, national brands may enter the field.

OTHER NICHES

Ancillary cannabis-connected businesses include real estate, consulting, lawyering, accounting, insurance and real estate services, packaging, payment processing, marketing, and security. This book does not address these niches.

Lecture Eleven: Hemp

Colorado is just starting its experiment with industrial hemp production, but interest in the new crop is so strong that the state is moving to expand the number and size of farms that can grow cannabis's non-intoxicating cousin.

A bill that won unanimous approval in a Senate committee will allow year-round hemp cultivation in greenhouses and put a 10-acre limit on hemp for research and development.

"Hemp, I believe, is going to be the most valuable crop for Colorado farmers in the future," said Michael Bowman, a farmer from Wray who plans to grow hemp on his eastern Colorado farm this spring. Others shared Bowman's enthusiasm.

"Hemp can fix every problem in the world if we just let it, so let's get to work finding out the hundreds of thousands of uses for hemp," said Sen. David Balmer, R-Centennial.

In 2011, the U.S. imported $11.5 million worth of hemp products, largely from China and Canada, compared to $1.4 million in imports in 2000. Most of that was hemp seed and hemp oil, used in granola bars, soaps, lotions and cooking oil.

Colorado authorized hemp cultivation in 2012 when it legalized marijuana for recreational use. Twelve other states have removed barriers to hemp production: California, Kentucky, Indiana, Maine, Montana, Nebraska, North Dakota, Oregon, Utah, Vermont, Washington and West Virginia.

The bill's passage appears likely, but there are obstacles to making hemp more than an experimental crop.

While a national Farm Bill signed into law in February lifts a decades-old ban on hemp cultivation, Federal law still bans importing hemp seeds which are considered a necessary for the industry.

In February, Colorado Gov. John Hickenlooper wrote to U.S. Agriculture Secretary John Vilsack seeking permission to import seed from other countries. "Our fear is that this seed shortage will unreasonably suppress the number of registered growers, stifling the wishes of Colorado voters to begin hemp production," Hickenlooper wrote.

State officials say that the USDA referred questions about hemp seed to the U.S. Drug Enforcement Administration. "What we've been told is that DEA trumps all," Ron Carleton, deputy agriculture commissioner and overseer of the industrial hemp program, told state senators.

Colorado's Agriculture Department has received 43 applications to grow hemp. Applications are being accepted through May. Farmers accepted into the program must test plants to make sure they are low in THC, the chemical that gives marijuana psychotropic effects.

Colorado currently requires hemp to be grown outside. Now state officials want greenhouse growing. "We can essentially grow it year-round when you do it indoors," Carleton said.

Once the hemp is harvested, the next step in the process is a little unclear, state officials say. Finished hemp can be legally exported out of state, but what that means is unclear. But can farmers send hemp seeds to another state to be turned into oil, or must the oil be produced in Colorado before it can be used in another state? No one has the answer as of this writing. "If we waited for Congress or DEA to do any of this, we'd all grow old, and the next generation would be sitting here having this conversation again," Bowman said.

Lecture Twelve: Direct Public Offerings

If a marijuana business files a state level registration that includes a formal offering document, such as a SCOR disclosure statement, it can make an exempt 504 intrastate public offering in more than one state. These offerings can be for up to $1,000,000, usually in two or more states that compose one of the five national regions the SEC has designated for this purpose.

Both the federal exemption and the state filing limit the raise amount to $1,000,000 in a one year period; a follow up offering cannot be made for 6 months.

Unlike other public offerings, 504/SCOR offerings have few onerous restrictions. General solicitation is permitted and there are no restrictions on type or number of investors. The SCOR filing is an actual registration, not an exemption. The form used is uniform so essentially the same form can be completed and submitted to each state. As of this writing, the following states do NOT accept a SCOR filing: Hawaii, Alabama, Florida, Delaware, Kentucky, and New York.

Most other states are "merit review" states. The following merit review states have a reputation for being less tolerant in their review of SCOR filings: California, Massachusetts, and Texas. The following states have a reputation for being more tolerant in their review of SCOR filings: Arizona, South Carolina, Iowa, and Washington.

The following states do not conduct a merit review: Connecticut, Georgia, Illinois, Maryland, New Jersey, Vermont, and Washington. In these states, the offering will be automatically approved as long as all the state forms are completed.

A start-up or other small business may want to offer securities only in the non-review states and the "more tolerant" states, if practicable.

These offers are sometimes known as direct public offerings (DPOs) or "self-underwritten" offerings. Agents and finders are permitted. Any type of advertising directed to any level of investor is permitted. The investor can invest as much as he wants.

SCOR in the Western States

Coordinated Review/SCOR/West CR-SCOR-West is a program for issuers of Private Issuers Public raisings (PIPRs) and others to sell equity securities in multiple Western states under SCOR/504 or SCOR/Regulation A.

This process coordinates registration in all of the states in the region. Eleven western states are currently participating in the program. California has a separate application process. States currently participating in the CR-SCOR-West program are Alaska, Arizona, Colorado, Idaho, Montana, Nevada, New Mexico, Oregon, Utah, Washington, and Wyoming. Colorado does not review Regulation A filings, so it participates only insofar as 504/SCOR filings are concerned.

Arizona and Washington have a reputation as being progressive toward SCOR filings in general. California, with its own manner of coordinating SCOR filings, is viewed as being often hostile to SCOR filings.

CR-SCOR-West is only available to SCOR/504 and SCOR/Regulation A (Model A or Model B) offerings.

- **Forms:** The issuer submits to each state in which it wishes to register the forms required by that state. These typically include the Form U-1 (Uniform Application to Register Securities); the Form U-2 (Uniform Consent to Service of Process); the Form U-2A (Uniform Form of Corporate Resolution); the Form CR-SCOR-West-1 (Application for CR-SCOR-West); and a copy of the completed /SCOR Form or Form 1A (PDF) and exhibits.

- **Financial Statements:** The CR-SCOR-West states differ in their requirements. For offerings of $1,000,000 or less, most states do not require reviewed or audited financial statements, but simply use generally accepted accounting principles (GAAP) with appropriate footnotes. Other states in the region require compliance with NASAA's Policy Statement Regarding Small Company Offering Registrations, which requires at least reviewed and, in some cases, audited financial statements. For offerings in excess of $1 million all states require audited financial statements.

Lecture Thirteen: Rule 506(c)

Many companies raise capital to start or expand operations by selling stock or debt securities, after finishing their "friends and family" round of financing. These offerings are regulated by federal and state securities laws which require registration. Since registration is costly and time-consuming, many offerings are made pursuant to exemptions to registrations, using private placements. Marijuana start-ups and other firms commonly rely on the exemption found in Rule 506 of Regulation D under the federal Securities Act of 1933, and on corresponding exemptions under state securities laws, for a "safe harbor" from registration. Effective September 23, 2013, new Rule 506 (c) allowed entrepreneurs to make use of general solicitations to sell securities for the first time in 80 years. And Rule 506(c) puts no limit on the amount of funds you can raise from friends, family, *and* strangers.

The SEC added provisions to restrict those with a history of regulatory issues. These "bad actor" provisions preclude general partners, managing members, executive officers, promoters or other representatives participating in a 506 offering (as well as anyone who owns 20% of the company) who have been convicted of any felony or misdemeanor involving securities or who is guilty of certain SEC regulatory matters.

Under Rule 506 (c), you can now advertise an offering using general solicitation, including use of websites and online advertising; electronic mail; social media, such as Facebook and Twitter, and all other online venues, as well as press releases; television; radio; direct mail marketing; and rolodexes.

You should have a process in place to communicate with possible investors. It may be helpful to say in your initial response that an intermediary, such as Private Placement Advisors, will be engaged to assist with distributing and collecting investor questionnaires and determining whether potential investors will qualify to purchase the securities you are offering.

If you are offering securities pursuant to a general solicitation, you can only *sell* them to "accredited investors." (You can *offer* them to anyone). Individual investors are accredited investors if they have either:

Net worth of at least $1 million, excluding the value of primary residence, or, Income of at least $200,000 in each of the last two years (or $300,000 with a spouse), and have the expectation to earn at least the same amount in the current year.

Other, less common, types of accredited investors can include a corporation; business trust; trust or partnership, not formed for the specific purpose of purchasing your company's stock or other securities, with total assets in excess of $5,000,000; an investment company registered under, or a business development company as defined in, the U.S. Investment Company Act of 1940; a Small Business Investment Company licensed by the U.S. Small Business Administration under Section 301(c) or (d) of the U.S. Small Business Investment Act of 1958; a private business development company as defined in the U.S. Investment Advisers Act of 1940; an entity in which all of the equity owners are accredited investors; an ERISA employee benefit plan if the plan has total assets in excess of $5,000,000 or if the investment decisions are made by a plan fiduciary that is a bank, savings and loan, insurance company or registered investment advisor; or self-directed employee-benefit plans that are controlled by an accredited investor.

Selling securities to non-accredited investors can result in an automatic right of rescission, a permanent future status as a "bad actor," and other penalties. You must take reasonable steps to verify that the each purchaser is an accredited *investor*. Issuers using a third-party verification service should initially respond to inquiries with a form letter that identifies the various categories of accredited investor and suggests a time and opportunity for a telephone conversation. A subsequent letter should describe the services of the verification and intermediary service you have chosen.

The accredited investor certifications required by the SEC depend on the status of each investor. An investor often qualifies under more than one test. The verification tests below appear in order of ease of effort under most circumstances. Many investors qualify under more than one test; always choose the least intrusive and most expeditious test(s) whether or not you use a verification service.

Income Verification

Individual earns more than $200,000 a year or $300,000 with spouse

Net Worth Verification

Investor is an individual with more than $1 million in net worth, excluding residence

Asset Verification

Investor is an entity with more than $5 million in good will or assets

Look-Through Verification

Investor is a member of an entity all of whose members are accredited investors

Entity Verification

Investor is a member of a special type of qualifying regulated entity

Affiliate Verification

Investor is a director, executive officer or general partner of a qualified issuer

Whichever certification you select, you must have policies in place to protect confidential information of potential investors and ensure compliance with all applicable privacy laws and regulations. Alternatively, you can use an accredited investor verification service that has these policies in place such as Private Placement Advisors, LLC.

You should use professionally prepared offering documents that describe:

a) The type of security your company is offering (limited partnership interests, limited liability company interests, promissory notes, common stock, etc.);

b) The price of the security;

c) The terms and economic rights such as dividends or interest payments, anti-dilution protections, and grounds for exemption from registration; and

d) Representations about the investors' accredited investor status; and

e) You must provide investors with annual reports or financial statements (or reasons not to have such documents) as well as a private placement memorandum, describing your company and its business operations and setting forth risk factors such as your limited operating history; risks related to the industry in which your company operates; risks specific to your company's products, technologies or services; and, finally, state that investors may lose their entire investment.

You also need to make sure to tell investors that because the securities were sold under the exemption in Rule 506(c), they are "restricted securities" and therefore re-sales are not permitted for six months.

A closing will occur when the investor delivers the purchase price and you issue the securities to the investor pursuant to the terms of the subscription agreement. You may decide to hold one closing or you may hold multiple closings throughout a pre-determined period of time.

You will need to make informational filings with the SEC and also with one or more state regulators after the closing. Although the securities sold under Rule 506(c) will be "covered securities" -- meaning state securities registration requirements are preempted by federal laws – you or a qualified intermediary, such as Private Placement Advisors, will need to make periodical, informational filings with each state regulatory authority in all states where the investors have a primary residence. Since each state has different filing requirements and some states have pre-filing requirements. It is helpful to know where each investor resides before any securities are sold, if practicable.

Appendix: The Cole Memorandum

U.S. Department of Justice

Office of the Deputy Attorney General

February 14, 2014

SUBJECT: Guidance Regarding Marijuana Related Financial Crimes

On August 29, 2013, the Department issued guidance (August 29 guidance) to federal prosecutors concerning marijuana enforcement under the Controlled Substances Act (CSA). The August 29 guidance reiterated the Department's commitment to enforcing the CSA consistent with Congress' determination that marijuana is a dangerous drug that serves as a significant source of revenue to large-scale criminal enterprises, gangs, and cartels. In furtherance of that commitment, the August 29 guidance instructed Department attorneys and law enforcement to focus on the following eight priorities in enforcing the CSA against marijuana-related conduct:

- Preventing the distribution of marijuana to minors;
- Preventing revenue from the sale of marijuana from going to criminal enterprises, gangs, and cartels;
- Preventing the diversion of marijuana from states where it is legal under state law in some form to other states;
- Preventing state-authorized marijuana activity from being used as a cover or pretext for the trafficking of other illegal drugs or other illegal activity;
- Preventing violence and the use of firearms in the cultivation and distribution of marijuana;
- Preventing drugged driving and the exacerbation of other adverse public health consequences associated with marijuana use;

- Preventing the growing of marijuana on public lands and the attendant public safety and environmental dangers posed by marijuana production on public lands; and

- Preventing marijuana possession or use on federal property.

Under the August 29 guidance, whether marijuana-related conduct implicates one or more of these enforcement priorities should be the primary question in considering prosecution under the CSA. Although the August 29 guidance was issued in response to recent marijuana legalization initiatives in certain states, it applies to all Department marijuana enforcement nationwide. The guidance, however, did not specifically address what, if any, impact it would have on certain financial crimes for which marijuana-related conduct is a predicate.

The provisions of the money laundering statutes, the unlicensed money remitter statute, and the Bank Secrecy Act (BSA) remain in effect with respect to marijuana-related conduct.

Financial transactions involving proceeds generated by marijuana-related conduct can form the basis for prosecution under the money laundering statutes (18 U.S.C. §§ 1956 and 1957), the un-licensed money transmitter statute (18 U.S.C. § 1960), and the BSA. Sections 1956 and 1957 of Title 18 make it a criminal offense to engage in certain financial and monetary transactions with the proceeds of a "specified unlawful activity," including proceeds from marijuana-related violations of the CSA. Transactions by or through a money transmitting business involving funds "derived from" marijuana-related conduct can also serve as a predicate for prosecution under 18 U.S.C. § 1960. Additionally, financial institutions that conduct transactions with money generated by marijuana-related conduct could face criminal liability under the BSA for, among other things, failing to identify or report financial transactions that involved the proceeds of marijuana-related violations of the CSA. *See, e.g.,* 31 U.S.C. § 5318(g). Notably for these purposes, prosecution under these offenses based on transactions involving marijuana proceeds does not require an underlying marijuana-related conviction under federal or state law.

As noted in the August 29 guidance, the Department is committed to using its limited investigative and prosecutorial resources to address the most significant marijuana-related cases in an effective and consistent way. Investigations and prosecutions of the offenses enumerated above based upon marijuana-related activity should be subject to the same consideration and prioritization. Therefore, in determining whether to charge individuals or institutions with any of these offenses based on marijuana-related violations of the CSA, prosecutors should apply the eight enforcement priorities described in the August 29 guidance and reiterated above.

For example, if a financial institution or individual provides banking services to a marijuana-related business knowing that the business is diverting marijuana from a state where marijuana sales are regulated to ones where such sales are illegal under state law, or is being used by a criminal organization to conduct financial transactions for its criminal goals, such as the concealment of funds derived from other illegal activity or the use of marijuana proceeds to support other illegal activity, prosecution for violations of 18 U.S.C. §§ 1956, 1957, 1960 or the BSA might be appropriate.

Similarly, if the financial institution or individual is willfully blind to such activity by, for example, failing to conduct appropriate due diligence of the customers' activities, such prosecution might be appropriate.

Conversely, The Department of the Treasury's Financial Crimes Enforcement Network (FinCEN) is issuing concurrent guidance to clarify BSA expectations for financial institutions seeking to provide services to marijuana-related businesses. The FinCEN guidance addresses the filing of Suspicious Activity Reports (SAR) with respect to marijuana-related businesses, and in particular the importance of considering the eight federal enforcement priorities mentioned above, as well as state law. As discussed in FinCEN's guidance, a financial institution providing financial services to a marijuana-related business that it reasonably believes, based on its customer due diligence, does not implicate one of the federal enforcement priorities or violate state law, would file a "Marijuana Limited" SAR, which would include streamlined information.

Conversely, a financial institution filing an SAR on a marijuana-related business it reasonably believes, based on its customer due diligence, implicates one of the federal priorities or violates state law, would be label the SAR "Marijuana Priority," and the content of the SAR would include comprehensive details in accordance with existing regulations and guidance because financial institutions are in a position to facilitate transactions by marijuana-related businesses that could implicate one or more of the priority factors, financial institutions must continue to apply appropriate risk-based anti-money laundering policies, procedures, and controls sufficient to address the risks posed by these customers, including by conducting customer due diligence designed to identify conduct that relates to any of the eight priority factors. Moreover, as the Department's and FinCEN's guidance are designed to complement each other, it is essential that financial institutions adhere to FinCEN's guidance. Prosecutors should continue to review marijuana-related prosecutions on a case-by-case basis and weigh all available information and evidence in determining whether particular conduct falls within the identified priorities.

Selective Glossary

Cannabidiol (CBD) is one of at least 60 active <u>cannabinoids</u> identified in <u>cannabis</u>. It is a major constituent of the plant, accounting for up to 40% of the plant's extract, as a non-<u>psychotropic</u> <u>phytocannabinoid</u>. It is considered to have a wider scope of medical applications than <u>tetrahydrocannabinol</u> (THC). Pharmacologically, the principal <u>psychoactive constituent</u> of cannabis is <u>tetrahydrocannabinol</u> (THC); it is one of 483 known compounds in the plant, including at least 84 other <u>cannabinoids</u>, such as <u>cannabidiol</u> (CBD), <u>cannabinol</u> (CBN), <u>tetrahydrocannabivarin</u> (THCV) and <u>cannabigerol</u> (CBG).

Cannabis is often consumed for <u>its psychoactive and physiological effects</u>, which can include heightened mood or euphoria, relaxation, and an increase in appetite. Unwanted side-effects can sometimes include a <u>decrease in short-term memory</u>, dry mouth, impaired motor skills, reddening of the eyes, and feelings of paranoia or anxiety.

Contemporary uses of cannabis are as a <u>recreational</u> or <u>medicinal</u> drug, the earliest recorded uses date from the 3<u>BC</u> . Since the early 20th century cannabis has been subject to <u>legal restrictions</u> with the <u>possession</u>, use, and sale of cannabis preparations containing psychoactive cannabinoids currently illegal in most countries of the world; the <u>United Nations</u> has said that cannabis is the most-used illicit drug in the world. In 2004, the United Nations estimated that global consumption of cannabis indicated that approximately 4% of the <u>adult world population</u> (162million people) used cannabis annually, and that approximately 0.6% (22.5 million) of people used cannabis daily.

Cannabinoids are a class of diverse chemical compounds that act on cannabinoid receptors on cells that repress neurotransmitter release in the brain. These receptor proteins include the endocannabinoids (produced naturally in the body by humans and animals), the phytocannabinoids (found in cannabis and some other plants), and synthetic cannabinoids (manufactured chemically). The most notable cannabinoid is the phytocannabinoid-tetrahydrocannabinol (THC), the primary psychoactive compound of cannabis. Cannabidiol (CBD) is another major constituent of the plant, representing up to 40% in extracts of the plant resin. There are at least 85 different cannabinoids isolated from cannabis, exhibiting varied effects.

Synthetic cannabinoids encompass a variety of distinct chemical classes: the classical cannabinoids structurally related to THC, the nonclassical cannabinoids (cannabimimetics) including the aminoalkylindoles1 1,5-diarylpyrazoles, quinolines, and arylsulphonamides, as well as eicosanoids related to the endocannabinoids.

The **Controlled Substances Act (CSA)** was passed as Title II of the Comprehensive Drug Abuse Prevention and Control Act of 1970 and signed into law by President Richard Nixon. The CSA is the federal U.S. drug policy under which the manufacture, importation, possession, use and distribution of certain substances is regulated. The Act also served as the national implementing legislation for the Single Convention on Narcotic Drugs.

The legislation created five Schedules (classifications), with varying qualifications for a substance to be included in each. Two federal agencies, the Drug Enforcement Administration and the Food and Drug Administration, determine which substances are added to or removed from the various schedules, though the statute passed by Congress created the initial listing, and Congress has sometimes scheduled other substances through legislation such as the Hillory J. Farias and Samantha Reid Date-Rape Prevention Act of 2000, which placed gamma hydroxybutyrate in Schedule I. Classification decisions are required to be made on criteria including potential for abuse (an undefined term) currently accepted medical use in treatment in the United States, and international treaties.

Hashish, often known as **hash**, is a cannabis product composed of compressed or purified preparations of stalked resin glands, called trichomes. It contains the same active ingredients—such as THC and other cannabinoids—but in higher concentrations than un-sifted buds or leaves.

Hashish may be solid or resinous depending on the preparation; pressed hashish is usually solid, whereas water-purified hashish—often called "bubble melt hash"—is often a paste-like substance with varying hardness and pliability, its color most commonly light to dark brown but varying toward yellow/tan, black or red. It is consumed by being heated in a pipe, hookah, bong, bubbler, vaporizer, hot knife (placed between the tips of two heated knife blades), smoked in joints, mixed with cannabis buds or tobacco, cooked in foods or smoked as bottle tokes ("brewing bots").

Hashish use as a medicine and recreational drug dates back to at least the 33rd millennium BC.

Kief (sometimes transliterated as keef or kif) refers to the resin glands (or trichomes) of cannabis which may accumulate in containers or be sifted from loose dry cannabis flower with a mesh screen or sieve. Kief contains a much higher concentration of psychoactive cannabinoids, such as THC, than that of the cannabis flowers from which it is derived.

Traditionally, kief has been pressed into cakes of hashish for convenience in storage, but can be vaporized or smoked in either form. According to the Oxford dictionary, the word "kif" derives from Arabic: كيف kayf, meaning well-being or pleasure which might come from the euphoric feeling caused by THC.

Tetrahydrocannabinol (THC) is the principal psychoactive constituent (or cannabinoid) of the cannabis plant. First isolated in 1964, in its pure form, by Israeli scientists Raphael Mechoulam and Yechiel Gaoni at the Weizmann Institute of Science, it is a glassy solid when cold, and becomes viscous and sticky if warmed. A pharmaceutical formulation of (−)-*trans*-Δ⁹-tetrahydrocannabinol, known by its INN, dronabinol, is available by prescription in the U.S. and Canada under the brand name Marinol. An aromatic terpenoid, THC has a very low solubility in water, but good solubility in most organic solvents, specifically lipids and alcohols.

Like most pharmacologically-active secondary metabolites of plants, THC in cannabis is assumed to be involved in self-defense, perhaps against herbivores. THC also possesses high UV-B (280–315 nm) absorption properties, which, it has been speculated, could protect the plant from harmful UV radiation exposure.

About the author

After getting a JD from Stanford Law School, a MA from the University of Chicago, a diploma from the University College London, and working as a reporter for The Wall Street Journal, Doug was a member of the California bar for 40 years, during which time he founded a series of law reporting services now owned by Thomson-Reuters. Doug specializes in debt and equity crowdfunding. He helps small business identify and solicit sources of private equity. Doug monitors a LinkedIn discussion group, State Securities Regulation, with 1500 members.

Connect with Douglas Slain:

LinkedIn: http://linkedin.com/in/douglasslain

Facebook: http://facebook.com/douglas.slain

Twitter: https://twitter.com/exemptofferings

Blog: http://www.privateplacementadvisors.com/apps/blog

Web site: http://privateplacementadvisors.com

www.ingramcontent.com/pod-product-compliance
Lightning Source LLC
Chambersburg PA
CBHW081758170526
45167CB00008B/3238